MODERN WORLD NATIONS

MODERN WORLD NATIONS

The Netherlands

ISCARD

James F. Marran
New Trier Township High School
Winnetka, Illinois

DISCARD

Series Consulting Editor
Charles F. Gritzner
South Dakota State University

CHELSEA HOUSE
PUBLISHERS
A Haights Cross Communications Company

Philadelphia

Frontispiece: Flag of the Netherlands

Cover: Kinderdijk Windmill, the Netherlands

CHELSEA HOUSE PUBLISHERS

VP, NEW PRODUCT DEVELOPMENT Sally Cheney
DIRECTOR OF PRODUCTION Kim Shinners
CREATIVE MANAGER Takeshi Takahashi
MANUFACTURING MANAGER Diann Grasse

Staff for NETHERLANDS

EXECUTIVE EDITOR Lee Marcott
PRODUCTION ASSISTANT Megan Emery
PICTURE RESEARCHER 21st Century Publishing and Communications, Inc.
SERIES DESIGNER Takeshi Takahashi
COVER DESIGNER Keith Trego
LAYOUT 21st Century Publishing and Communications, Inc.

A Haights Cross Communications ◤ Company

http://www.chelseahouse.com

First Printing

1 3 5 7 9 8 6 4 2

Library of Congress Cataloging-in-Publication Data

Marran, James F.
   The Netherlands / by James F. Marran.
      p. cm. -- (Modern world nations)
Includes index.
Contents: Introducing the Netherlands -- Natural landscapes -- The Netherlands through
time -- People and culture -- Government -- Economy-- Living in The Netherlands
-- The Netherlands look ahead.
   ISBN 0-7910-7476-5
 1. Netherlands--History--Juvenile literature. 2. Netherlands--Social life and customs--
Juvenile literature. 3. Netherlands--Description and travel--Juvenile literature. 4.
Netherlands--Geography--Juvenile literature. [1. Netherlands.] I. Title. II. Series.
DJ18.M34 2003
949.2--dc21

                                                                        2003007318

Table of Contents

MODERN WORLD NATIONS

The Netherlands

Windmills and water are two common sights throughout the Netherlands. For hundreds of years, the Dutch used windmills to drain water from the land.

1

Introducing the Netherlands

*I*n the beginning, the place was a swamp on the banks of the North Sea that later became an empire. That is how the famous historian and geographer Hendrick Willem van Loon described the Netherlands for a world history he wrote in the early 20th century. The description was apt even though a bit harsh, perhaps even cruel. The Netherlands is an appropriate name for a small and tidy country tucked neatly on the shores of the North Sea between Belgium and Germany, because it is indeed a nether, or low, place. In fact, about two-thirds of the country is below the level of the sea.

The Netherlands literally means "low land." In earlier times when most of Europe was still unsettled, the name meant exactly what it implies—a low, remote, and distant place on the edge of the continent. This low-lying land is laced by three unruly rivers—the Rhine, the Scheldt, and the Maas—all of which empty into the North Sea.

In France where the Maas begins, it is called the Meuse. Today, the people of the Netherlands have tamed the rivers and transformed them into essential arteries of trade in Northern Europe. In ancient times, however, these unpredictable waterways, plus the fury of the North Sea, often kept much of the land from 2 to 16 feet (.60 to 4.9 meters) below water. In those days, the Netherlands really lived up to its name.

The constant challenge to people who settled in this difficult environment was the same as it is today. To survive, the Dutch (as the people who live there are called) must tame the rivers and hold back the great tides of the North Sea behind dunes, sea walls, and embankments known as dikes. For centuries, the Netherlands was at the mercy of nature. A single flood could be catastrophic, wiping out whole cities, towns, and villages. Overnight, thousands of people could be swept away by the power of the flooding rivers and the thunderous sea tides.

Such an unpredictable physical geography makes the often-told story of the heroic little Dutch boy believable. On his way home one evening, he found a leak in a dike. Knowing that the small leak could rapidly expand and become a flood, he quickly put his hand in the hole to plug it. He stayed there all night until some farmers found him in the morning and mended the leak. The boy's steadfastness saved the day, and his courage and persistence became a symbol of the watchfulness that all those who live in the flood-prone Netherlands must possess.

In modern times, Dutch engineers have tamed nature with massive flood control projects. These include reinforced dikes, concrete dams, sand dunes, and an elaborate drainage network of canals throughout the country. In the past, thousands of windmills harnessed the power of the wind to drive the pumps that kept this lowland country from flooding. Today, however, electric motors power most of the pumps. The windmill, once a symbol of the Netherlands, is a relic of the past.

The Dutch have become experts at designing ways to reclaim land from the sea. Almost two-thirds of the

Netherlands, including all the country's main population centers, was at one time below water. The drained areas of land created by the near magic of technological achievements are called polders. These drained acres have become the richest and most productive farmlands in the Netherlands, and home to hundreds of thousands of people.

Indeed, what for centuries was the country's greatest weakness proved to be its greatest strength. As an old Dutch saying recalls, "God created the world, but the Dutch created their own place on Earth." From the marshes and swamps along the North Sea, and from the unchecked flow of their rivers, the Dutch gradually brought order out of nature's chaos. No longer are the Dutch subject to the whim of the waters that surround them. Now secure behind seawalls and other water barriers, the Netherlands is one of the wealthiest nations in Europe. A leader in banking, high-tech industries, agriculture, and trade, the country plays a key role in world commerce. Rotterdam, which controls the mouth of the Rhine River, is the world's largest seaport. It helps connect much of Europe to the rest of the world. Adding to the city's importance is a collection of docks, warehouses, and ship-turning basins that line the shores of the delta waterways from the city to the North Sea. Called the *Europoort*, its massive size and complexity help make Rotterdam a major contributor to the powerful Dutch economy. Because of its location at the juncture of the Rhine and the North Sea, the Netherlands is called the gateway of northern Europe.

A LONG AND VARIED HISTORY

The modern Netherlands was born in the 1600s after centuries of conflict with its European neighbors. With its independence established, the Dutch entered a period of prosperity called the Golden Age. The Netherlands became a major sea power, competing with Spain, Portugal, England, and France for trading rights and claims to lands in Asia, Africa, North America, and the Caribbean. Gradually, it commanded an extensive colonial empire that included possessions in nearly every part of the globe. Dutch ships brought the wealth of the world back to Amsterdam, a city that had become one of Europe's great trading centers, and the most important city in the Netherlands.

In the 1600s, the Dutch East India Company (1602) and the Dutch West India Company (1621) were organized to expand trade and promote good relations between the government and its overseas colonies. Their phenomenal success rivaled similar enterprises organized by France and England. In many instances, they were more profitable largely because they were authorized to exercise administrative and judicial power as well as to conduct trade. The administrative skills of the Dutch, their efforts at neutrality, and their reputation for fairness and integrity earned them respect in areas of the world where other colonial powers were sometimes viewed with suspicion. As a result, they were invited to trade with Japan, which had isolated itself from the rest of the world. In Japan, the Dutch set up wharves and established a trading post on a small island in the harbor of Nagasaki where they conducted a highly profitable enterprise for over 200 years.

From the sixteenth century to the early nineteenth century, the Dutch enjoyed power and prosperity all over the world. Success abroad brought success at home. With the patronage of businessmen and other wealthy citizens, art, scholarship, and innovation flourished. Dutch painters, for example, created pictures of stunning magnificence. Some of these artworks were portraits of the rich and powerful, while others were of ordinary people in the elegant simplicity of everyday life. Exquisite scenes of Dutch landscapes and seascapes captured the beauty of the countryside and the unpredictability of the North Sea.

Cartography, or mapmaking, had become important, too. The accuracy and artistry of Dutch maps were second to none in the world. Maps were the emblems of empire. The Dutch prominently and proudly displayed them in their homes, shops, counting houses, and banks. Better maps encouraged more ambitious trading ventures. These, along with new navigational instruments and improved sailing ships, made travel easier and safer, and also assured an increase in the volume of commerce. Dutch ships were a common sight in all the world's ports.

With its prosperity, Dutch society became the most open and the most tolerant in all of Europe. That remains true today. As a result, the country served as a haven and a refuge for political and religious dissenters who had been forced to leave countries that had little tolerance for those who challenged the established ways. One such group was the Puritans from England who spent almost 10 years in Leyden, a small city of weavers and printers in the west of the Netherlands. Concerned that their children were becoming more Dutch than English, they decided to leave and sail to America in search of religious and political freedom in 1620.

Ultimately, however, long and costly wars with England and France exhausted the Dutch. Their quest for empire ended in the early 1800s when French Emperor Napoleon Bonaparte's troops invaded the country and forced a Dutch surrender. Left weak and ineffectual, the Netherlands lost most of its overseas possessions and was forced to assume a secondary role in the European family of nations. By the mid-1800s, however, the political situation in the Netherlands had stabilized. The Dutch once more enjoyed a period of commercial expansion in world markets and internal developments at home. Important reforms were introduced that resulted in a more stable government and an improved quality of life for the Dutch people. At the start of the twentieth century, the Netherlands had quietly moved to a position of industrial and economic strength. At home, its house was in order and many of its imperial holdings in East Asia, Africa, and in the Caribbean had been renewed.

STRUGGLES OF THE TWENTIETH CENTURY

With the coming of the twentieth century, the future was full of promise. By the end of the century, however, the Dutch had endured two world wars and periods of economic depression

The Netherlands' location makes it an easy transfer point for shipments in and out of Europe. Because of its location at the juncture of the Rhine and the North Sea, the Netherlands is called the gateway of northern Europe.

and uncertainty. In both wars, they declared their neutrality. The Germans respected that declaration in World War I, but not in World War II. In the early days of the fighting in 1940, German bombers destroyed most of Rotterdam and wreaked havoc on the canals and dikes everywhere. The Dutch learned that they were vulnerable. For the remainder of the war, they were brutally occupied. By the time the Germans surrendered in 1945, the Netherlands was in ruins and the Dutch people had suffered greatly.

At the end of the war, the Dutch and the other Low Countries (Belgium and Luxembourg) agreed to form a union called the Benelux Economic Union to use their collective energies to rebuild. Although the union was never fully successful, the Dutch learned a valuable lesson. They realized that they could gain strength through economic and defense alliances with the other nations of Europe.

Since the end of World War II, the Dutch have prospered. They have reestablished trade and built a respected international banking system. They have also benefited greatly from the discovery of large natural gas deposits in the North Sea that have proved to be a huge economic gain. Chemical and microelectronics industries flourish and Dutch-produced flower bulbs (including the famous tulips), fresh flowers, and food reach markets in virtually every country. Today, the Dutch are an affluent people who are often characterized as conventional and conservative, but whose outlook on the world is positive and optimistic.

To better understand this remarkable country, one must understand its physical geography. With its small size, limited resources, and difficult physical environment, the natural landscape provides the setting for the country's extraordinary cultural achievements throughout history. Knowing Dutch geography is the key to understanding how the Netherlands became the home of an industrious people who reclaimed much of their homeland from the sea.

The landscape of the Netherlands is laced with many navigable rivers and canals. These waterways serve as vital transportation routes.

2

Natural Landscapes

Although small in comparison to most other countries, the Netherlands is full of surprises. It extends only 180 miles (290 kilometers) north to south and 120 miles (193 kilometers) from the shore of the North Sea on the west to the German border in the east. From top to bottom, a person can drive through the Netherlands in about four hours, the same driving time it takes to travel between New York City and Washington, D.C.; Chicago and St. Louis; or Seattle, Washington and Portland, Oregon.

Low and flat as the Netherlands is, the landscape is not at all monotonous. In fact, it is quite varied. It supports a great many types of activities, from farming and horticulture to modern industries, and from high stakes banking and financial services to tourist facilities. Even though the country is, on average, only 40 feet (12 meters) above sea level (which means that much of it rests on the former floor of the North Sea on polder lands), the Dutch have fashioned a remarkable country that contains great natural and cultural diversity.

A DECEPTIVE CLIMATE

The country's absolute location is between 53° and 55° north latitude. Without any intervening circumstances, that means it ought to have long, cold winters and short, cool summers. It would be the kind of weather expected by people who live in northern Siberia or the Canadian tundra, because these places are at approximately the same latitudinal location as the Netherlands. In spite of its position within Earth's higher latitudes, however, the climate in the Netherlands is unexpectedly moderate. *Temperate* is the best word to describe the fairly mild and damp conditions that are common year-round. That is because it is in a climate zone called west coast marine. Westerly winds blow in off the Atlantic Ocean, carrying moist air to the Netherlands and other coastal areas of northwestern Europe.

In the United States, the Pacific Northwest has a similar climate. It also occurs in coastal southern Chile and in almost all of New Zealand. In the case of the Netherlands, the warm waters of the Gulf Stream heat air masses that hover over the Atlantic Ocean. In the northern Atlantic, this current is known as the North Atlantic Drift. It carries warm water from the tropics near the Equator almost as far north as the Arctic Circle, but it has a very moderating effect along the way. Extremely hot or cold temperatures are rare in the Netherlands. Winter skies are generally overcast, with foggy days common all year long. Warmer winters mean there is very little frost. Summer is the wettest season, but precipitation is fairly evenly distributed throughout the year. Most of the country receives an average annual rainfall of 30 inches (76 centimeters). Because there are few natural barriers, such as high mountains, the climate in the Netherlands varies little.

A NATION OF REGIONS

As is the case with every other part of Earth's surface, the Netherlands is best understood by studying its physical regions. A region is an area that shares common features or characteristics that distinguish it from surrounding areas. Just as historians divide time into eras, such as the Middle Ages or the Renaissance, geographers divide the world into regions.

Understanding the regions of a country makes its landscape easier to appreciate because the patterns of similarities and differences can be seen. In the United States, for example, the Midwest is quite different from the Rocky Mountain region. The Midwest is generally flat with large, sprawling cities and thousands of acres of fertile farmlands crisscrossed by slow-flowing rivers and streams. The Rocky Mountains, on the other hand, are composed of high, snowcapped peaks with many rivulets tumbling off the mountainsides to the meadows below. In such an environment, cities are few and far between, and except for some cattle ranching and sheep herding in the lower elevations, agriculture hardly exists.

The Netherlands has the same kind of contrast as larger countries, although not quite as dramatic. It is divided into four main land regions stretching from the Southern Uplands near its border with Belgium to the Dunes that run almost the full length of the country along the North Sea coast. To the west is the Polders region that runs the length of the country, north to south. In the east, there is the Sandy Plains region, an area about 40 miles (64 kilometers) wide that also runs the breadth of the country, along the wavy and curly boundary the Netherlands shares with Germany. Altogether, these four regions define the Netherlands. Knowing the regions of the Netherlands provides a better understanding of the whole country.

Regardless of region, water is an ever-present reality in the Netherlands. Over the centuries, human intervention has played a key role in making the country habitable and manageable. In

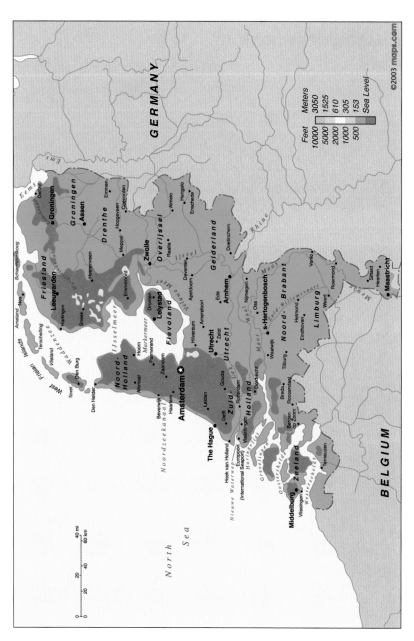

Low and flat as the Netherlands is, the landscape is not monotonous. Instead, it is quite varied and supports many diverse activities. The country, on average, is only 40 feet (12 meters) above sea level. Regardless of the region, water is an ever-present reality in the Netherlands. In every region, managing water is a priority and a necessity.

every region, water management is both a priority and a necessity. All people, regardless of age, occupation, or address, know that their survival depends on flood control.

The Southern Uplands

On a map of the Netherlands, a squiggle of land in the southeast corner of the country lies tight up against the Belgian border. It is here that the Meuse River takes on its Dutch name, the Maas, as it flows into the Netherlands from France and Belgium. The Maas marks part of the border between Belgium and the Netherlands on its journey to the North Sea. The region's largest city, Maastricht, is also the oldest in the Netherlands. It is a manufacturing, communications, and cultural center that also has a large butter market produced by the dairy industry in the surrounding countryside. This area constitutes the Southern Uplands and is about one-third the size of Rhode Island, the smallest state in the United States. The whole region is squeezed into Limburg Province, famous for the cheese it produces. Many people the world over insist that the cheese has such a strong odor, that it is often mistaken for old gym shoes.

Elevations in this region are the highest in the country. They rise to just over 1,000 feet (305 meters), which means that the region is hilly, not mountainous like the Alps or the Pyrenees of southern Europe. A better way to describe this landscape is to call it "rolling," because its hills gently unfold into fertile fields. Such an environment supports many highly productive dairy farms. Vegetables and fruits are also grown in abundance. Fields of white asparagus are harvested in late spring and grapes in the fall. Apple and cherry orchards are especially famous for the quality of the fruit they produce. They are what make the famous Dutch apple and cherry pies such tantalizing treats.

Because of the Roman influence in this region, many people claim Latin ancestry. Along with cross-border influences with the Belgians and the Germans, this makes the Dutch of this region a bit different in style and outlook from their countrymen in the north and west. The location of the Southern Uplands has made the region a European crossroads, and thus one of several areas of the Netherlands that enjoys a genuine international flavor.

The Dunes

The coastline of the Netherlands curves gracefully along the North Sea from the deltas of the Rhine and its two river neighbors, the Maas and the Scheldt in the south, northward to the West Frisian Islands. Along the narrow beaches lies a long line of sand dunes. Although none reaches more than 100 feet (30 meters), the dunes play a crucial role in the life of the country. The dunes are the first line of defense against the fierce storms and tidal surges that rage in from the sometimes unpredictable North Sea. The sea is the region's weather maker, often disturbing the sunbathers and beachcombers who enjoy the coast's sandy expanse and the challenge of dune-climbing on summer days.

Over thousands of years, the action of the currents and the constantly blowing westerly winds of the Atlantic Ocean resulted in the buildup of a huge sandbar along the coast of Northern Europe. Gradually, the bar fractured to become the barrier dunes that line the Dutch shore today. Some of these sand hills were occasionally broken by river outlets flowing across the flat plain in the north of Holland (another name for the Netherlands), or by the impact of violent sea storms.

At the north end of the coastal crescent defined by the dunes, sit the West Frisian Islands. Once part of the Dutch mainland, the power of the North Sea long ago divided the sandbar into these low-lying islands. They are now separated from the Netherlands by the shallow Waddenzee (meaning "muddy sea" in Dutch). The five West Frisians are part of a

The long coastline of the Netherlands is a favorite vacation spot for the Dutch and tourists alike.

larger archipelago (chain of islands) whose other islands belong to Germany and Denmark.

For centuries, the islanders made their living fishing and raising sheep and cattle. These activities still go on today. The islands are home to the largest cattle market in Europe, but tourism is now the major industry. Vacationers come by the thousands each year to visit the nature preserves and ecological habitats set aside by the Dutch government. Many also stay to enjoy the beaches and *wadlopen*, the art of wading thigh-high in mud from the mainland across the Wadden Sea. As much fun as this might be, a sudden change in the weather, including a fast approaching sea storm, can make mud-wading a dangerous activity. Another popular activity is *fierljeppen*. Originally a method used by farmers to help manage their fields and pastures, vacationers pole vault like circus acrobats across the islands' many canals.

The Polders

The polder region, so fascinating to visitors to the Netherlands, lies immediately to the east of the narrow string of dunes. Polders are lands reclaimed from the sea that are protected from flooding by dikes and gigantic electric pumps that operate day and night. The polder lands exist because of the skill of Dutch engineers and the intricate drainage system they have devised.

Thousands of years ago, violent storms, sudden floods, and uncertain tides from the North Sea constantly threatened the early settlers of Holland's northwest. To protect themselves, the settlers built their dwellings and buildings astride large earthen mounds called terpens. These became havens in times of natural disaster, when the sea exploded with tidal surges, winds, and heavy rains. To assure further protection, early settlers constructed dikes connected by roadways to join the terpens. Although the enclosed land was generally safe from flooding, it had to be drained, since much of it was below sea level. Over hundreds of years, the Dutch improved the drainage techniques so that, by the 1400s, windmills pumped water higher and higher into rings of canals that carried the water to the sea via a series of channels. As a result, it was possible to drain increasing amounts of land below sea level. Today, the process remains much the same, except the technology is more sophisticated. Many of the polders are as much as 20 feet (6 meters) below sea level. Dikes, pumps, small lakes, and canals protect more than half the country.

Polder projects are as much a part of the history of the Netherlands as was the Dutch success as sixteenth-century traders and empire builders in Asia, Africa, and the Americas. A good example is the project, completed in 1932, in which the government finished an 18-mile (29-kilometer) dike enclosing

This dike road separated the Zuider Zee from the North Sea. The dike also links North Holland to Friesland, a northern province of the Netherlands.

the Zuider Zee, a long arm of the North Sea. The purpose of the dike was to separate the Zuider Zee from the North Sea and make it a freshwater lake. The new lake that resulted was named IJsselmeer because it was fed by the IJssel River. The project permitted the drainage of more than half a million acres (202,343 hectares) of reclaimed land to be used for settlement and agriculture.

In spite of the security promised by IJsselmeer, a devastating flood occurred in 1953. It killed almost 2,000 people, destroyed thousands of homes and businesses, and caused millions of dollars in damage, including the destruction of much of the polder land. In response, the Dutch government launched the ambitious Delta Project in 1958. Completed in 1986, the idea was to rearrange most of the delta area around the Rhine and other nearby rivers to stem the constant threat of the North Sea storms and tides. Planners shortened the coastline by more than 400 miles (644 kilometers) by constructing three massive sea dams, a system of dikes and bridges, a network of locks for ship access to the sea, and a major canal. The dikes created many freshwater lakes with causeways joining some of the offshore islands. Since its creation, the size of Lake IJssel has increased because of the volume of fresh water from the Rhine and other rivers in the country.

The reclaimed polder land is an important resource for the Dutch. Millions of people live in the region in large urban areas surrounded by some of the country's most productive farmland. Dairy meadows and farms are common, and so are tulip and hyacinth bulb fields. After being harvested, the bulbs are shipped to places in the temperate zone all across the Northern Hemisphere. Each spring, the flowers brighten the day with a dazzle of color.

The Sand Plains

The vast European Plain starts its sprawl eastward at the lip of the North Sea in the Netherlands and continues its way across Germany and Poland to the Ural Mountains in Russia. The low-lying land in eastern Holland, with its ridges and rolling landscape, is typical of the plain. Millions of years ago, the receding glaciers of the last ice age deposited the sandy soil common to the region. Heath lands, moors, and small forests are common in this region. One of the largest and most beautiful conservation areas in Europe is located here as a national park.

Although much of the soil is not very fertile because of its excessive sand content, fertilizers make farming possible. In fact, the region has become quite agriculturally productive. There are many orchards, small farms, and acres of glistening greenhouses where flowers, fresh fruits, and vegetables are cultivated year-round. Most of this produce is exported to markets in Europe and North America. It is in this region, too, that the Rhine River enters Holland on its way through Rotterdam and on to the North Sea. Its tributaries and the canals that lace the area are vital arteries of trade, linking farms and cities with the rest of the country and the world beyond.

During the 1600s and 1700s, the Dutch fought the British for control of the seas. Although the Dutch won many battles, constant warfare left the Netherlands weakened and the British eventually triumphed.

3

The Netherlands Through Time

I t took a long time for the Netherlands to become an independent country. In part, this was because of its remote location on the northwest fringes of Europe. It was also partly the result of the power vacuum left after the collapse of the Roman Empire in the fifth century A.D. Along its way to becoming a nation state, the Netherlands was ensnared by invaders and foreign armies of occupation, by distant monarchs eager to expand their realms, and by religious conflict resulting from the Protestant Reformation.

The earliest historical accounts of the Netherlands date from the first century B.C., when Roman soldiers led by Julius Caesar conquered the Germanic and Celtic tribes living in the area. Even then, managing the waters of the rivers and the North Sea was the key to survival in the region. To make the land habitable, Germanic Batavi people drained the marshes and lagoons in the Rhine Delta. Farther north, Celtic Frisians built the terpen mounds on the islands and sandy coastal flats of the North Sea. These separate efforts created the earliest polders.

This was the era of *Pax Romana* ("Roman Peace"), a time when Roman rule brought stability to all parts of the empire, which included the upper Rhine River valley. It lasted for more than 250 years. Tranquillity ended sometime around A.D. 400, when strong and well-organized tribes invaded from the east. The Franks, among the most powerful of these tribes, fiercely subdued the land's inhabitants. Frankish missionaries converted the conquered people to Christianity, establishing a rule of law that had been missing in Europe since the fall of the Roman Empire.

On Christmas Day, 800, Charlemagne, strongest of all the Frankish kings, was crowned Holy Roman emperor by the pope in Rome. The coronation was full of fanfare and pageantry, and it marked the transfer of power from the Mediterranean world, where it had been centered since ancient times, to Europe and the Atlantic. A new world order was established, and the countries of Europe—including the Netherlands—would be key players on the world stage. The Holy Roman Empire, however, was fragile. Too much land stretching over a whole continent made the emperor's one-person government impossible. Control of outlying regions was difficult to maintain, because roads were poor and communications were primitive. To fill the gap, a system of land ownership called feudalism developed. This was a complicated legal and social arrangement in medieval Europe where powerful lords granted lands to nobles in exchange for the promise of military service. Land was worked by serfs, whose poverty-stricken lives resembled the condition of slavery. At the top of the chain of command was the Holy Roman emperor, but too often, his power was more theoretical than actual. For almost 500 years, the chaotic Europe of the Middle Ages struggled for order.

After the death of Charlemagne, the Frankish kingdom

weakened and fractured into three parts. In a now disjointed Europe, the Dutch faced tremendous difficulties. Their political future was uncertain and they continued to struggle against the sea. Worse, they faced a new threat from a group of powerful Scandinavian seafarers: the Vikings. These invaders terrorized the coasts of Northern and Western Europe. For 200 years, the Dutch fell prey to their vicious and unpredictable raids.

The attacks ended only when the Dutch fortified their towns, and were thus able to repel the assaults. These towns, built to stop the Viking marauders, gradually grew into important trade centers where merchants and skilled craftsmen developed an economic system that challenged feudalism. Many also became university and cathedral towns. What resulted was an improved quality of life for the *burghers*, the middle-class townspeople who were developing capitalism. This was a new economic system based on free enterprise, built on investment and designed to bring in profits.

PASSING OF THE MIDDLE AGES

By 1200, Western Europe was ready to erupt with reckless energy and move beyond the disruption of earlier times. New ideas and technologies were about to challenge the dominant role of the established Roman Catholic Church, which for almost 1,000 years controlled all aspects of daily life, including art and learning. The Netherlands was an integral part of that authority. In the Middle Ages, the Church and European civilization were one.

A major challenge to the power of the Catholic Church came from the Renaissance and the rise of humanism. These two movements rediscovered the power of Greek and Roman ideas. Writings about philosophy, law, and science developed by ancient Greek and Roman authors were translated at new universities founded all over Europe. One of the most prestigious of these universities was Leiden in the Netherlands.

Scholars found new ways to look at the world and its problems. Gradually, every aspect of medieval life was called into question, including the Church itself. From 1517 on, Martin Luther, a German monk, argued that Church reform was necessary. He even challenged the authority of the pope, the bishop of Rome. Many Christians believed that the popes were the successors to Peter, the chief of the Apostles of Jesus Christ and the first bishop of Rome. A central theme of the Protestant Reformation that followed was the new belief that knowledge of the Bible was the only thing necessary for a person's soul to be saved. Doing good works and helping others did not matter. This position was a stunning departure from Church doctrine that had long taught that faith based on the Bible and good works were both needed for salvation.

Luther's radical ideas were attractive to the freethinking Dutch people, especially those in the northern part of Holland. Even more than Luther, they were interested in the teachings of John Calvin, a French reformer who lived in Geneva, Switzerland. Calvin amplified Luther's message in a carefully structured way, stating that God decided even before people were born who would enter heaven (and who would not), for reasons that humans could not understand. People could do nothing to change God's plan. Many people responded to this message of predestination with an intense moral fervor, especially in the market towns and cities of Holland. Many of the Dutch became avid Calvinists. Even though people could never be sure that God had chosen them to be saved, they tried to live in such a way as to appear to be among the elect. It took hard work and an effort to be successful. The new Dutch burghers embraced this teaching and created a prosperous society built on self-reliance and personal responsibility.

One of the effects of Calvinism in Holland was the importance placed on tolerating diverse opinions. The Dutch valued freethinkers who challenged traditional ways of looking at things. Such open-mindedness made their country a sanctuary for Jews, Huguenots (sixteenth and seventeenth-century French Protestants), and other dissenters from across Europe.

These refugees enriched Dutch life in a number of ways. They helped make the Netherlands one of Europe's most powerful and most enlightened countries as it embarked upon a race for empire in the sixteenth century.

Of all the vehicles of change that brought a new order to Europe, none was more powerful than the printing press. Developed in the mid-1400s by the German inventor Johann Gutenberg, the printing press made the exchange of information far more efficient than ever before. Not only could religious writings be easily circulated, but so could travel reports, maps of faraway lands, and woodcuts showing scenes and everyday objects of newly discovered places. The Dutch quickly adopted this new technology and became among the best-informed people in Europe.

Nowhere else in the world during these centuries was change greater than in Western Europe. The Dutch played a key role in putting aside the old ways. They accepted new forms of religion, developed efficient ways of doing business, designed strategies to manage the threat of war, and sent their well-armed vessels to Africa, Asia, and the Americas in search of territory and trade opportunities. No assumption went unexamined. No opportunity was spurned. The Dutch were inventing a future of promise, but competition from their equally ambitious neighbors posed ominous threats.

NETHERLANDS BECOMES A WORLD POWER

The Netherlands has always been a country of limited resources. As a result, the Dutch have been forced to do more with less. Their most abundant resource, of course, is water. It seems to be everywhere. It is both a curse and a blessing: a curse because of its destructive power; a blessing because it has connected the country to world markets and made the Netherlands one of the great maritime nations in modern history. That leadership role, however, did not go unchallenged. When the Dutch were moving to the peak of their power in the seventeenth century, they were threatened by Spain, France, and Britain, each being anxious to overtake them.

In the early 1500s, the Dutch came under Spain's control. The Dutch conversion to Calvinism infuriated the king of Catholic Spain. To crush them, he sent his armies to the Protestant provinces to force their return to Catholicism. He was partially successful in the southern provinces, but not in the seven northern ones. There, a Dutch nobleman named William the Silent, prince of the House of Orange, led a successful rebellion. The determined Dutch resistance forced the Spanish to abandon their garrisons and retreat south. By 1581, an independent Netherlands, known as the United Provinces, emerged.

Victory gave the Dutch control of the Rhine River delta and the estuary of the Scheldt River. That guaranteed the security of their ports, especially Amsterdam, which had become a major city. The merchant marine flourished, with Dutch ships trading throughout much of the world. They even had exclusive commercial rights in such faraway countries as Japan. With a virtual monopoly on trade and the successful settlement of several overseas colonies, Dutch burghers became enormously wealthy.

DECLINE OF DUTCH POWER

To protect their supremacy and extend their trade around the world, the shrewd Dutch negotiated an alliance with Britain and Sweden in 1668. Its larger purpose was to curb the growing influence of Louis XIV, France's powerful and sometimes ruthless monarch. The alliance so infuriated King Louis that in 1672, he sent French forces to overrun and occupy the Netherlands. Desperate, the courageous Dutch opened their dikes and dams, flooding much of the country and making it impenetrable to the French army. The victory, however, was costly. The country was all but ruined and the economy derailed. Only the important concessions the Dutch won at the peace table allowed them to rebuild.

The success of the Dutch was short lived. Over the next few

William the Silent (1533 – 1584) led a rebellion to free the Netherlands from Spain. The Dutch call him the "Father of the Netherlands."

decades, more wars followed in the constant clashes among the European powers for control of the world's oceans and the acquisition of colonies. It was a great war for empire.

The British, especially, had designs on the Netherlands. They wanted to destroy its sea dominance, crush its trade, and conquer its colonies. Their mission was to sink the Dutch. As a result, there was a series of bitterly fought naval engagements during the next century. Ultimately, the Dutch triumphed, but they were badly weakened. Two centuries of warfare against the Spanish, French, and British brought the Netherlands to the point of collapse. The religious wars resulting from the Protestant Reformation also took their toll. The Dutch had overextended themselves everywhere. Industry and trade were weakened, and the economy was in tatters.

The final blow came in June 1786, during the last of the Anglo-Dutch wars. After a fierce four-day battle in the Strait of Dover off the English coast, the Dutch fleet was destroyed. Thousands of sailors perished along with hundreds of their officers. The economic loss was no less tragic than the human one; the Dutch fleet was destroyed and the country's overseas trade was paralyzed. At home, the wharves were empty, making the port cities no longer centers of commerce. Holland had become a second-rate power.

In 1795, the weakened and impoverished Dutch fell to the French army under Napoleon Bonaparte. He renamed the country, appointed his younger brother king, and set up a new government. At the same time, the British seized most of the Dutch overseas empire.

By the early 1800s, with the fading of Napoleon's power and staunch Dutch opposition, French rule came to an end. In its place, the United Kingdom of the Netherlands was born. The kingdom included Belgium and Luxembourg, Holland's Low Country neighbors. The first king, William I of Orange, was crowned in 1814. The House of Orange rules to this day, but only with limited power. Union with Belgium and Luxembourg, however, did not last because of differences in language, religion, and culture. Both went their separate ways as independent states, leaving the Kingdom of the Netherlands to the Dutch.

THE DUTCH IN THE MODERN WORLD

In the nineteenth century, the Netherlands became increasingly more stable and overcame the disruption caused by earlier European wars. The government was more democratic, expanding the right to vote and providing improved social services in education, health care, housing, and other quality of life issues. As demand for social reform increased, the Dutch enjoyed economic expansion as the country moved into the twentieth century. Its overseas trade flourished and its colonies in Asia and the Caribbean were restored to play an important role in the life of the country.

That prosperity was cut short, however. With the outbreak of World War I (1914–1918), the Dutch suffered great hardship, despite their declared neutrality. The naval blockade of Europe, enforced by the British and their allies to weaken Germany and shorten the war, placed heavy burdens on the Dutch. Isolated and alone, their trade and shipping came to a standstill.

After the war, the resilient Dutch revitalized their economy. They also improved their country by constructing dams, dikes, and canals to further protect the coastal areas and the Rhine delta from the destructiveness of North Sea tides and floods.

A troubled and uncertain peace followed World War I. There was a worldwide economic depression with unemployment, poverty, and economic collapse almost everywhere. Soon, war drums were again beating in Europe as some nations began huge military build-ups. Dictators such as Adolf Hitler in Germany and Benito Mussolini in Italy had plans to conquer Europe and dominate the rest of the world. When war came in 1939, the Dutch once again declared their neutrality, but the Germans still invaded. In four terrifying days, German bombers destroyed much of Rotterdam, while the German army inflicted heavy damage on the rest of the country.

The war years (1939–1945) were among the most difficult in Dutch history. German occupation was a time of widespread terror, with mass executions of resisters and the deportation of almost all Jews to death camps in Poland. The German siege was both destructive to the physical environment and devastating to national morale. Queen Wilhelmina, the reigning

During World War II (1939–1945), German bombers destroyed much of Rotterdam. This photograph was taken after the debris was cleared. All that is left of entire streets is the foundations of the buildings.

monarch, and her government fled in exile to London. Misery and deprivation paralyzed Dutch life. Only the hope of an Allied victory kept the country from despair.

When Allied troops routed the German army in May 1945, the queen and her cabinet immediately returned to the Netherlands. Later that year, the Netherlands became a charter member of the United Nations (UN) and began the hard work of building a future. As a founding member of the European Common Market and the North Atlantic Treaty Organization (NATO), the Netherlands became a significant force in molding a new Europe.

In the postwar era, the Dutch successfully rebuilt their country and restored trade and industry. Holland is now one of the most technically advanced countries in Europe, employing millions of people in service occupations with worldwide connections. International trade in manufactured goods and agricultural products is vital to the country's success in the global economy.

With a future firmly rooted in its past, the Netherlands moves into a new century committed to its traditions of enlightened trade policies and intelligent statesmanship. Its aim is to be a creative force in the global economy that grows more and more interdependent. The Dutch recognize that a new spirit of cooperation has replaced the competition with European neighbors so characteristic of earlier times. They are among the continent's most ardent advocates for a United States of Europe.

Erasmus Bridge is one of many expressions of modern architecture found in Rotterdam. The city was rebuilt after its destruction during World War II.

CHAPTER

4

People and Culture

A lthough the population of the Netherlands is small by most standards, it is one of the most densely populated countries in the world. In Europe, only Monaco and Malta have a greater number of people per square mile. About 40 percent of the Dutch live in cities of 50,000 or more, mostly in the western part of the country along the North Sea. One region includes Amsterdam, The Hague, Rotterdam, and several other cities that together create an area known as the *Randstad*, or "ring city." All the land area is below sea level, requiring planned and controlled drainage before anything can be built. This horseshoe-like arrangement of connected cities is clustered around a still-rural center comprised of some of the world's most productive farmlands and market gardens.

Even though there are boom cities in other parts of the Netherlands, the *Randstad* dominates the Dutch economy and

Dutch culture. Each city that is part of the Randstad plays a special role. Amsterdam, the largest, is the cultural and financial focal point of the Netherlands. Located on the Amstel River, it is both the constitutional capital and a busy commercial port that specializes in international trade and light manufactured goods. Many of its neighborhoods are home to thousands of immigrants from former Dutch colonies, such as Surinam and Indonesia. In addition, many guest workers from Turkey, Eastern Europe, and Morocco also live in these neighborhoods. In many ways, these people have changed the face of the Netherlands as their traditions blend with traditional Dutch culture.

Rotterdam is the world's busiest seaport. This is largely due to its location in the Rhine delta on Europe's threshold. In recent years, however, Singapore, Los Angeles, and other cities have challenged Rotterdam's dominance as its output of heavy industries declines and its regional economy becomes more service-oriented. Rotterdam must also cope with increased competition from other European ports that challenge its longtime advantage of location. In spite of these challenges, however, energetic and boisterous Rotterdam is still where freight traffic converges from the oceans of the world and from the canal and river systems of Europe. This has made the Dutch essential to the commercial stability of the continent.

The Hague is quite different. It is the "gracious lady" of the Netherlands, seat of the Dutch government, where the reigning monarch lives, and site of the United Nations' International Court of Justice. This court was the brainchild of Dutch law professor Tobias M.C. Asser (1838–1913). He was a leading advocate for world peace and spent much of his life working to achieve it by designing ways to resolve conflicts among nations as alternatives to war. It was his work that resulted in a Permanent Court of Arbitration. For his efforts, he received the Nobel Peace Prize in 1911. Asser's collaborator was Andrew Carnegie (1835–1919), the enormously successful American industrialist who developed the steel industry in the United States. Through the Carnegie Endowment for World Peace, founded in 1910, Carnegie provided funding to build the Peace Palace, the permanent home of the Court since World War I. Carnegie wanted an international court of justice to be his legacy, and he chose The Hague as its site. In addition to a number of important government buildings, the city also has many museums celebrating Dutch art and other achievements.

The phenomenon of the Randstad is not confined to the Netherlands. The reality of the megalopolis (super city) is increasingly evident throughout the world. Nearly all of the rapid urban growth is the result of rural-to-urban migration, people moving to cities in search of better lives. As more and more of these megacities develop in every part of the world, many planners look to the Dutch for models that provide an efficient and comfortable quality of life. The Randstad is a prototype of an urban agglomeration. It is a collection of parklands, spacious and well-developed housing subdivisions, reliable communication networks, and an affordable public transportation system. Yet these features are all connected in a huge urban mass that is the core of the country.

GETTING AROUND AND KEEPING CONNECTED

Holland's intense urbanization has created rural areas that are never remote, but only less densely settled extensions of the cities. Scarce land means small farms. Two-thirds of the country's area is given over to grazing animals and crop production in fields or in row upon row of greenhouses. Most farms are only about 35 acres (14 hectares). They are intensely cultivated, using modern agricultural methods and heavy amounts of chemical fertilizers. This helps make them the source of high-quality fresh produce and dairy products sought in markets throughout the world. Fresh flowers of virtually every variety are also in great demand. In the spring, lush gardens of tulips, daffodils, and hyacinths are everywhere. Flowers are commonplace in shops, and brighten the many overcast days the North Sea brings. Dutch flowers also grace homes, hotels, and restaurants from Madrid to Memphis to Melbourne every season of the year.

Because of the high population density (over 1,000 people per square mile, compared to about 79 in the United States), most people in the Netherlands own bicycles. The flat landscape makes bicycles easy to manage so they have become an important means of transportation for people of all ages in every part of the country. Without bicycles, life would often be at a standstill because heavy traffic congestion on narrow streets and roads frequently creates gridlock. Cycling is also an important recreational activity with rallies, races, and relays common on holidays and weekends. Champion bike racers are as popular among the Dutch as major league baseball players are among Americans.

As much as the Dutch people might seem alike because of their country's size and urban orientation, they have clear differences, especially when it comes to religion. Those living in the north in the Randstad tend to be Protestant and generally more reserved than those in the Catholic south, who are more outgoing and gregarious. In recent years, however, secularization, or the diminishing importance of religion in national life, has lessened the presence of religion among the Dutch regardless of the regions where they live.

IMPORTANCE OF FAMILY AND PERSONAL VALUES

In cities or on farms, the core of Dutch life is the family, a closely-knit unit that serves as the center of social activity. Family members enjoy visiting one another for meals and family parties where they share leisure activities. The family circle is where Dutch cultural values are transmitted from one generation to the next. These include committing oneself to productive work, building strength of personal character,

Bicycles are one of the most common forms of transportation in the Netherlands. These bicycles are parked near a waterway in Amsterdam.

developing attitudes of tolerance and understanding, and appreciating family loyalty.

These values complement an outlook on life that is straightforward and practical. The Dutch are not demonstrative in public situations, and appear quite reserved, even formal. With family and friends, however, they are relaxed and good-humored. Caring and warmth characterize their relationships.

First time visitors to the Netherlands are always impressed with the sense of order they find. Regardless of region, everything is well organized and well planned with an emphasis on neatness and cleanliness. The Dutch appreciate structure and bring logic to every aspect of their lives. They are also personally modest and prudent, frowning on displays of wealth.

Simplicity is a virtue they cherish. What results is a disciplined society that is objective in outlook and tolerant of differing points of view.

THE DUTCH LANGUAGE

Standard Dutch is the official language of the Netherlands, and is spoken by about 20 million people worldwide. Although the language is closely related to German, it has a very different sound. Words careen off into unusual vowel formations that seem to clatter when they thud and bounce against diphthongs and consonants. The government also recognizes Frisian as an official language in the northwestern province of Friesland. Its origins are Old English, the language used by Geoffrey Chaucer when he wrote *The Canterbury Tales* in fourteenth-century England.

As one of the less widely used languages in Europe, Dutch is under threat of gradually disappearing. English is spoken with increasing frequency throughout the country, especially in business communication. More than three-quarters of the Dutch use a second language. English is by far the most popular, but German is also frequently used.

DAILY LIFE

The Dutch enjoy life and live it to the fullest. Their year is a cycle of family gatherings, holiday get-togethers, and sporting events in which everyone is included. One of the most important holidays is Queen's Day, celebrated each year on April 30. It is much like the Fourth of July in the United States, but it honors the memory of Queen Wilhelmina, who became the symbol of Dutch resistance against the German occupation of Holland during World War II. All across the country, there are games, parades, picnics, and flea markets. Many towns and big city neighborhoods organize *kermis*, fairs that feature carnival attractions with shows, rides, and food booths.

Food is important in the Netherlands. For families, it is a

social experience, and on an everyday level, it helps define the rhythms and patterns of life. A typical breakfast includes cheese, bread, and cold meat with hot chocolate or coffee. Lunches are usually sandwiches or light salads. Dinner, the main meal of the day, is more hearty. Meat or fish with potatoes and vegetables are favorites, but *hutspot* is a national specialty. It is a tasty meat stew laced with potatoes and fresh vegetables, steeped in rich gravy. Most Dutch also enjoy raw herring amply sprinkled with onions and spices, often accompanied by thin pancakes, smothered with a variety of toppings. In recent years, this substantial fare has been joined by the immigrant foods brought by Indonesians and other groups living in the Netherlands. Their spices and lighter ingredients have changed Dutch cooking and influenced Dutch tastes.

Even though food is an important part of Dutch culture, people enjoy recreational and sporting activities as well. Boating, sailing, and wind surfing are popular sports on the country's many rivers, lakes, and canals. Swimming and sun bathing are also favorite summer pastimes on the sandy beaches along the North Sea. In local communities, numerous sports clubs organize various seasonal sports for young people and adults. The most popular are field hockey, soccer, cycling, and tennis. When winter weather permits, however, ice-skating tops them all.

DUTCH ART: A NATIONAL TREASURE

Of all the achievements of the Netherlands, none is more reflective of its culture than the work of Dutch artists in the Golden Age of the seventeenth century. Museums the world over prize their work, and paintings from this period are always in great demand. Their power is in their simplicity. They depict scenes of the commonplace, showing ordinary people going about the business of their lives. Paintings show women cleaning their homes and preparing food, men at work in their shops, the stock exchanges and counting houses, children at play, and family members enjoying one another's company. Each picture is a moment frozen in time portraying the day-by-day scenes of the prosperous Dutch whose newfound wealth permitted them the luxury of supporting painters and buying pictures for their homes and workplaces. Most of these artworks were small compared to the massive art of the Middle Ages and the Renaissance, but they were attractive because they were relevant to people's lives.

As ordinary as such paintings appear today, in their own time they were revolutionary. Almost all were a departure from the highly formalized styles of earlier artists who typically depicted scenes from the Bible or the ancient myths of Greece and Rome. Such innovative art was possible after Holland freed itself from Spanish domination in 1609. Organized as the United Provinces, the new nation was ready to explode into a period of unprecedented economic growth after decades of foreign control. The resulting success made the Netherlands one of the wealthiest and most powerful nations in the world for the next two centuries.

Cities were the centers of this prosperity. Some city dwellers were highly skilled as goldsmiths, diamond cutters, and cloth and spice merchants. Others were involved in enterprises based on trade in distant ports. There were also people in more commonplace but no less essential occupations. These included bakers, cobblers, blacksmiths, and shopkeepers. In the energetic urban settings of Amsterdam, Rotterdam, The Hague, and Utrecht, open dialog in the coffee houses, guildhalls, and market stalls was necessary for successful business transactions. These conversations often led to discussions on other topics as well. Some were challenging, even controversial. What resulted was an open society where tolerance for divergent viewpoints made the United Provinces unusual in Europe at that time.

Most citizens in the United Provinces were Protestant, and they placed a priority on learning to read and write. Protestants understood that literacy was essential to understand

and interpret the Bible, which was an important part of their religion. A number of books were published on biblical subjects. In time, however, some books began to go beyond religion to inquiries on astronomy, geography, mathematics, civics, and anatomy. These works encouraged further investigations in the newly opened schools and institutes.

In the spirit of a society that encouraged innovation, artists whose work had been limited to mystical and supernatural subjects were eager to create canvases that were daring departures from traditional themes. In addition to scenes of the domestic world that the Dutch cherished, artists painted landscapes depicting the details of actual places for the first time. Human portraits were also a favorite. These paintings, showing affluent burghers and their families, offered insights into the daily lives of the Dutch. They are also powerful testaments to the artists' creative genius.

A constant thread through all these works of art was a fascination with light and shadow. Dutch painters saw in every subject such infinite possibilities for expression that each painting was an experiment with the power of illumination and color. That sense of exploration defines Dutch art from that day to today.

Although scores of artists from the Golden Age ably captured the breadth of Dutch culture, a few are recognized the world over as genuine masters of their craft. One of the earliest of these artists was Hieronymus Bosch (1450?–1516), whose religious paintings were charged with depictions of fear and evil. His work presents images of Hell showing its grotesque distortions and people in the throes of great torment. As awful as they are, it is Bosch's courageous realism that distinguishes his work. His paintings deeply influenced the quality and style of art to come.

Rembrandt van Rijn (1606–1669), perhaps the best known of all Dutch artists, painted daring pictures on an array of subjects. Always disciplined and focused, he presented a world

Netherlands native Rembrandt van Rijn (1606–1669) was one of the world's greatest artists. He painted this self-portrait a few months before his death.

of stability and quiet grandeur. Subtle light became a magical ingredient in each of his paintings. His portraits are among the most insightful ever painted, because through them, he was able to capture the essence of each of his subjects and reveal the depth of their character. Frans Hals (1580?–1666) and Jan

Vermeer (1632–1675) are also well known, especially for how their works depict the details of everyday Dutch life—such as a woman sitting quietly at a table reading, a blacksmith laboring at his anvil, and a baby in its cradle, caught in the glimmer of sunlight. The legacy of such artists is the elegant record of Dutch life that their groundbreaking pictures have preserved.

The Dutch monarch is installed on the throne in an investiture ceremony.
This photograph shows the inauguration of Queen Juliana, who ruled from
1948 to 1980.

5

Government and Politics

The Netherlands has a monarch and a royal family where the oldest child succeeds the parent on the throne. This practice, which dates back to the Middle Ages, is called primogeniture. Although royalty reigns, the country is a democracy with a constitutional government directed by a prime minister and a parliament called the States-General that consists of two houses. This organizational structure makes the Kingdom of the Netherlands a constitutional monarchy similar to those in Belgium, Denmark, Norway, Sweden, and the United Kingdom.

The king or queen is head of state, but has very little power. The monarch's role is largely symbolic. The king or queen signs all the bills passed by the States-General, appoints key officials on the advice of various government agencies, and officiates at important social ceremonies and political functions. Under the Dutch system of checks and balances, the monarchy's role is minimal, but its presence is a special part of Dutch identity and deeply rooted in its history.

Unlike monarchs in many other countries, the new king or queen of the Netherlands is not installed on the throne by the nobility, the church, or the armed forces. Instead, the monarch is invested, indicating that the *people* bestow the power. Investiture takes place in Amsterdam, surrounded by much colorful pageantry. The tradition dates back to the Middle Ages, when the monarchy pledged to protect the rights of the subjects in exchange for recognition of its power. This symbolic act, affirming that a partnership exists between the king or queen and the people, has become an integral part of Dutch life.

PARLIAMENTARY GOVERNMENT

The primary source of law in the Netherlands is its constitution, written in 1814 and regularly updated to meet society's changing needs. A parliamentary system of government is the core of the constitution, with significant power resting in the two houses of the States-General. The 75 members of the First Chamber are elected to four-year terms by the 12 provincial legislatures. The Second Chamber is larger, with 150 members elected to four-year terms directly by the voters in each province.

Under the Dutch system, a number of political parties participate in the political process. Each represents a different philosophy of government, ranging from strong conservatives on the extreme right, to strong liberals on the extreme left. To acquire seats in the Second Chamber, a party must win a certain percentage of the votes cast in the general election. Such proportional representation assures that the Second Chamber's make-up will reflect the will of the people across the broad political spectrum.

The First Chamber has less power in public affairs than the Second Chamber, since only the Second Chamber can propose legislation. The monarch can also propose legislation, but only through the Cabinet, whose members are appointed by the prime minister to operate the government. Both chambers must approve bills before they can be signed into law by the monarch.

Since World War II, no single party has won enough seats to allow it to control the Second Chamber. That has meant the Netherlands was led by coalition governments in which all the political parties must compromise on issues relating to leadership and national priorities. Because there is no clear majority, one party usually dominates in such coalitions, or partnerships. For the most part, the dominant parties have been the Christian Democrats and the Labor Party. It is not uncommon for the prime minister and the Cabinet to disagree with the policies and programs endorsed by the States-General. When that happens, either the prime minister or the Cabinet will resign, or parliament will be dissolved and new elections held. Unlike the American president, the Dutch prime minister has no specific term of office. He or she serves only as long as the States-General offers its support.

Just as the Congress of the United States meets in the Capitol in Washington, D.C., the Dutch States-General also convenes in a designated building in The Hague. The Dutch capitol is called the *Binnehof* and was used by the counts of Holland in the 1300s as their royal court. Today, the striking and stately Binnehof is beautifully maintained as the home of the States-General. It serves as the centerpiece of the surrounding buildings that house government departments and offices.

To begin each newly elected parliament, the States-General convenes in joint session on the third Tuesday in September. The monarch presides after a ceremonial drive in a horse-drawn carriage through the crowd-lined streets of The Hague from the royal palace to the Binnehof. As part of the ceremony, the monarch addresses the members on the important issues facing the country. It is much like the State of the Union message that the president of the United States gives before Congress each January.

POLITICAL PARTIES

To Americans, whose political system is organized around two major parties, the Democrats and Republicans, Dutch politics might appear to be confusing because there are so many parties. Today, Holland boasts more than 30 of them. That is the reason coalition governments are common in the Netherlands.

In recent years, four parties have attracted the most votes, but never a majority. The Democrats 66 Party and the Labor Party take a liberal approach on issues such as health and child-care, workers' rights, education, and pensions. On the right is the conservative People's Party for Freedom and Democracy. It takes a more cautious view of government, working for lower taxes, limited regulation of the private sector in the Dutch economy, and less spending for social welfare programs. The Christian Democratic Appeal is the center, or moderate, party. Its leaders argue for a balanced approach to government by avoiding the extremes of the left and right. Many people believe that this party is much too tentative and indecisive on impor-tant issues to govern effectively.

Small parties are numerous and also important in the Dutch system, because they represent positions not always on the agenda of the larger parties. These groups often organize in response to a particular problem. As a result, they disappear as quickly as they form. Although a system that supports so many political parties might seem fractured to outsiders, to the Dutch it assures that every point of view has a voice in the political process and can have a place on the ballot.

Since becoming a fully independent country, the Netherlands has had many powerful and inspiring leaders whose vision has shaped Dutch politics. One of the best known is Pieter Jelles Troelstra (1860–1930). He was a social reformer whose influence reached far beyond his own country. Among his contributions, he founded a Socialist party advocating an eight-hour workday, the right of women to vote, improved wages

A Dutch woman casts her vote in the eastern village of Spakenburg. There are more than 30 political parties from which to choose in the Netherlands.

and conditions for workers, and abolition of the monarchy. Before his death, Troelstra won all but one of the causes he championed—the monarchy remained. It was too closely associated with the identity of Holland, and the members of the royal family were too highly respected for the system to be toppled. Affection for the monarchy continues today.

THE NETHERLANDS AND ITS COLONIES

In the era of European imperialism, no country was a more successful colonial power than Holland. Even though most of its possessions became independent after World War II, it still governs the Netherlands Antilles, also called the Dutch West Indies. These Caribbean possessions consist of two island groups. Bonaire and Curacao form the southernmost group, located off the coast of Venezuela. Here, refineries processing oil from Venezuela reship petroleum products to consumer nations in Europe and North America. This important economic activity brings in revenues exceeding one billion dollars a year to the local economy. Farther north, in the Lesser Antilles, are the small islands of Saba and St. Eustatius. These islands and the southern part of St. Martin, which also is controlled by the Dutch, are attractive tourist destinations. They are attractive because of their year-round warm climate, sandy beaches, and coral reefs for scuba divers.

Aruba, an island 40 miles (64 kilometers) off Venezuela, was a Dutch possession until its people voted to secede from the Netherlands in 1986. In 1994, however, they decided to indefinitely suspend transition to full independence. Now officials in The Hague manage the island's defense and conduct its foreign affairs. Aruba's government handles all internal matters. As is the case with Bonaire and Curacao, its main source of revenue is the refining and reshipment of petroleum. These few remaining overseas possessions are more like dependencies than colonies. They make limited contributions to the Dutch economy, and often they are even liabilities.

In the fifteenth and sixteenth centuries, the States-General chartered trading companies in the western Pacific Ocean and in North and South America to ensure a monopoly of trade for the Dutch government. The success of the Dutch East Indies Company and the Dutch West Indies Company made the Netherlands among the richest nations in Europe. The Dutch gained great wealth from their acquisition of the Indonesian archipelago, much of the Malaysian Peninsula, and other parts of Southeast Asia. They also gained control of Dutch Guiana (now Surinam), a number of Caribbean islands, and outposts in the Hudson River Valley in what is now New York State. Dutch power and influence seemed to be limitless, but did not go unchallenged by other European powers.

When the Dutch established government controlled trading

These Dutch colonial buildings on the Caribbean island of Curacao serve as a reminder that the Netherlands was once a major colonial power.

companies, they showed other European nations that the era of exploration (fifteenth to the eighteenth centuries) had moved from exclusively political goals to economic ones. The Dutch model of commercial monopoly was imitated by other nations, especially France, England, and Sweden. The driving force in this competitive area was mercantilism. Mercantilism was an economic theory that supported the establishment of colonies to supply raw materials, such as sugar, cotton, coffee, and tobacco, to be processed and marketed in exchange for gold. The goal of a successful mercantile nation was to build a system of colonies that would provide a yearly favorable balance of trade. That meant it would export more than it imported, and have surplus gold to either lend or invest in new enterprises.

By 1900, many people in the Netherlands were concerned over the moral and ethical implications of imperialism. They were concerned about fairness issues, the right of people to self-government, and the right of people to manage their own economies. The debate was intense. No firm consensus ever developed, even in the wake of pressure from the colonies themselves as they pressed for independence. The end of World War II, however, brought a turning point. The Dutch recognized the independence of the Dutch East Indies in 1949, after a four-year struggle to keep it a colony. With its independence, the former colony became the island country of Indonesia. Elsewhere, the Dutch transferred New Guinea to the United Nations in 1962, made Surinam a republic in 1975, and granted self-governance to the Caribbean island of Aruba in 1986. The legacy of Dutch imperialism means that former colonies have become independent nations, important in the world community.

THE DUTCH IN INTERNATIONAL AFFAIRS

After World War II, the European nations realized that they could no longer afford go-it-alone foreign policies. Cooperation and collective security were necessary if the new Europe emerging at war's end was to recover and prosper. Because the Netherlands had suffered so severely during the German occupation, the country was at the forefront in organizing the United Nations. It also became a charter member of this important international body. Their participation over the years has been significant. Dutch policy has consistently supported UN peacekeeping efforts, as well as its humanitarian programs for refugees and other dislocated people. The Netherlands continues to be a persuasive influence. The World Court, located in The Hague, demonstrates the unwavering commitment the country has had over the years in promoting order and justice within the international community.

The Dutch also played a key role in developing NATO in 1949. Initially, NATO was a military alliance of Western European and North American nations, structured to check the growing power of the Soviet Union and its satellites in Eastern Europe after 1945. Holland was one of the original members to join. The heart of NATO's mission is contained in Article 5 of its charter. It establishes that an attack against one member is an attack against all, and will result in a united response. Other articles commit members to build a common military force, strengthen their democratic institutions, and consult each other on issues of mutual concern. Members are also pledged to remain open to inviting other European nations to join.

Since the collapse of the Soviet Union in 1991, NATO membership has expanded. Poland, the Czech Republic, and Hungary are new members, and other Eastern European nations are likely to follow. In the post–Cold War era, NATO has pledged itself to a continuing dialog with its former enemies.

NATO has built its own military bases, airfields, supply depots, fuel pipelines, and communication networks throughout Europe. All are jointly funded and collectively maintained. There is even a strike force that can move quickly to any trouble spot, much like a SWAT team. With the Soviet Union and its allies no longer a threat, NATO continues to promote collective security by extending its role to contain conflicts on Europe's periphery. It played a key role in the war in the Balkan States of Serbia, Croatia, Kosovo, Bosnia, and Herzegovina in 1995. With the situation controlled, NATO set up a multinational force of peacekeepers of which soldiers from the Netherlands were a part.

Tulips are one of the Netherlands' most important agricultural products.
Fresh flowers are sent from fields like this one to markets all over the world.

6

The Economy

Since its emergence as a major power in the seventeenth century, the Netherlands has generally enjoyed a thriving economy. Initially, fishing and shipbuilding served as its basis, but as Dutch vessels sailed to foreign ports with goods to exchange, the country became a trading nation. Over the centuries, a strong merchant marine and an effective international banking system have evolved to keep the Dutch connected to world markets.

Trade is still an essential part of the modern Dutch economy, but today it is more diversified than in earlier times. With limited natural resources, the country is heavily industrialized. Its factories produce everything from steel and heavy machinery, to textiles and sophisticated electronic equipment. Most of what it makes is sold overseas. Agriculture also makes an important contribution to the national economy. Even though less than 5 percent of the work force is involved in farming, it consistently provides large quantities of produce and meat products for the food processing industry. The value of Dutch agriculture ranks third in the world after the United States and France. This figure is statistacally amazing, considering that the country's crop land occupies an area no larger than the tiny state of Rhode Island. Production of high-value specialty crops—including flowers, flower bulbs, fruits, and vegetables—accounts for the huge economic success of the agricultural economy.

A large reason for the prosperity of the Dutch economy has been due to its banking system. Amsterdam has long been one of the world's major financial centers, and it remains so today. A significant portion of the annual income of the Netherlands comes from the financial services it offers to the world community and from its role in foreign trade. In recent years, tourism has also become an important part of the economy. Quaint villages with their canals and windmills, the lure and excitement of the cities, and the country's many historical sites attract hundreds of thousands of visitors annually. Schipohl (pronounced *Shipull*), the huge international airport between Amsterdam and The Hague, provides easy access from cities in North America and all parts of Europe, North Africa, and the Middle East.

A SERVICE-BASED ECONOMY

The powerful economy of the Netherlands consistently places it in the top 20 of the world's most successful financial systems. Dutch commercial banks have large foreign operations, with branches worldwide to serve investors. In the last few decades, growth in financial services has outstripped every other area of the economy, including manufacturing. Over 60 percent of the work force is now employed in the service sector, with more than half providing banking, investment, insurance, real estate, and other financial services. Most of the remaining workers are in manufacturing, agriculture, and government.

The government is a supportive partner, working with the business community to promote economic stability through its tax and trade policies. It interferes as little as possible in the internal affairs of corporations and trade groups. The government also has played a leading role in the development of multinational organizations committed to reducing trade barriers and promoting international cooperation. The Netherlands belongs to a number of regional and global economic associations, demonstrating its role as a major player in the world economy. The balance that characterizes Dutch society has made its economic system widely regarded as a model of consensus between government and the private sector, resulting in a consistently high standard of living and a comfortable quality of life.

MINERAL RESOURCES

With so much of the country reclaimed from the sea, natural resources are very scarce in the Netherlands. Most raw materials needed for industry or domestic use must be imported. However, one resource found in abundance in the polder lands and the swampy areas along the North Sea coast is peat, partially decayed plants found in wet ground. When dried and processed, peat has many uses. Some is exported to less developed countries as an inexpensive and slow burning fuel. Industry uses it as an insulating material, while farmers use peat as a mulch and soil conditioner. The polders also have fertile soils, making them highly productive agricultural areas. In the southeast uplands in Limburg Province, there are coal mines, now largely inactive because the quality of the coal is poor and the veins thin. New fuel sources and improved technologies have made reliance on domestically produced coal unprofitable.

In 1959, large natural gas deposits were discovered in Groningen Province in the northwest Netherlands. Their volume now makes natural gas the country's most abundant natural resource. There is also some petroleum nearby, but its quantity has proved disappointing. Encouraged by the success of the British and the Norwegians in their search for oil, geologists had hoped to find large reserves in the North Sea. However, exploration of the Dutch waters produced only small yields of oil. Instead, they discovered additional rich natural gas deposits, the most abundant in Europe. As a result, there are very few offshore oil wells. Domestically refined petroleum meets less than 5 percent of the country's needs. But in Rotterdam, there are some of the world's largest refineries where crude oil from the Middle East and other sources is processed for fuel and industrial uses and shipped in super-tankers to overseas markets. Much fuel also goes by pipeline to industries in nearby Belgium and Germany.

Other mineral resources include salt, gravel, sand, and clay. However, such industries employ few workers and account for a very small percentage of the Gross Domestic Product (GDP) of the Netherlands. The GDP is the value of the goods and services produced within a country in one year. Goods are materials such as minerals, manufactures, flowers, and fresh produce, whereas services involve occupations where people help one another in such activities as finance, technology, retailing, and professions, such as teaching, medicine, and law.

MANUFACTURING AND AGRICULTURE

Industry and farming account for a notable portion of Holland's GDP, with most coming from manufacturing and food processing. Advanced technology, a well-educated and multilingual work force, and a flair for innovation and creativity have made the Dutch successful industrialists. The inventory of what they produce includes everything from cars, trucks, light aircraft, and chemicals to electronic appliances, complex medical laboratory equipment, and the most recent pharmaceutical breakthroughs. Many well-known international manufacturers have established their world headquarters in the Netherlands,

The modern Dutch economy manufactures many products, including medications. This pharmaceutical plant is located in the southern city of Geleen.

making it an important part of the globalization process as transnational corporations increasingly challenge the importance and relevance of national boundaries.

In an increasingly connected global economy, dairy products, chocolates, baked goods, and meats processed in the Netherlands are common in markets all over the world. The country is one of the largest cheese manufacturers, each year challenging Wisconsin to be the world leader. Dutch beer is popular as an adult beverage and is produced under many different brand-names. The food industry also includes fisheries. Herring and other ocean fish have long been an essential part of the Dutch economy. Boats in the Dutch fleet continue their regular runs in the North Sea and the North Atlantic harvesting fish for freezing and canning. This success in food production and processing is in large measure due to the flexibility of industry and the strength of Dutch agriculture. Together they have developed a highly mechanized and computer-driven system that enables them to respond to changing preferences and tastes both at home and overseas.

TRADE AND TRANSPORTATION

Trade has long been the lifeblood of the Netherlands. Without it, the country would perish. Major Dutch industries are those that export the highest percentage of what they produce. Typically, leading exports include fresh fruits and vegetables, processed foods, synthetic fabrics and fibers (including orlon and acrylon), chemical products, refined petroleum, and electrical and transportation equipment.

In spite of its enormous production capacity, the Netherlands is not self-sufficient. It depends on imports for materials it cannot produce itself. These commodities include grain used in food processing and as animal feed, crude petroleum, and such non-electrical equipment items as machine and automotive parts. The five most active Dutch trading partners are Belgium, Germany, France, the United Kingdom, and the United States. Together they account for more than 70 percent of the exports and about 60 percent of the imports. That creates a favorable balance of trade, meaning that annual exports exceed imports. What results is an annual profit for the Netherlands.

The country's advantageous location plus its well-developed network of waterways, highways, railroads, and pipelines make it an easy transfer point for shipments in and out of Europe. Rotterdam, with its pivotal location in the Rhine delta, is the key to the trading success of the Netherlands. The cargo unloaded there and transferred to the interior of Europe is three times as great as the amount loaded. This makes

Rotterdam the world's leading break-of-bulk point, meaning that cargo coming into Rotterdam is divided into smaller quantities and distributed by truck, rail, and barge to less dominant port cities in Europe and beyond.

THE EUROPEAN UNION

Once called the European Community (EC), the European Union (EU) is an international economic association founded in the 1990s to reduce trade barriers among European nations and to increase cooperation. As one of its founders, the Netherlands has played a central role in organizing and promoting more open trade policies among its European neighbors through the EU.

The history of the European Union began shortly after World War II. At that time, the Dutch urged economic unification as a means of preventing another war. In 1952, the Netherlands and 14 other countries joined to form the Economic Community. Within a few years, it became known as the European Common Market. A series of subsequent treaties have provided the building blocks for the foundation of a united Europe. The most decisive was the Maastricht Treaty on European Union signed in that historic Dutch city in 1992. It created a free trade association, a common currency (the euro), a European Central Bank, and a structure for managing the many aspects required for intergovernmental cooperation among member states. The euro replaced the Dutch guilder as the official currency of the Netherlands on New Year's Day, 2002. It also became the recognized monetary unit of most of the other members of the EU on that same day, assuring a standard unit of exchange among participants. The euro makes trade negotiations with non-members much less complicated than dealing with separate national European currencies.

There are 15 member states in the EU: Austria, Belgium, Denmark, Finland, France, Germany, Greece, Ireland, Italy,

In 2002, the Netherlands switched currency from the Dutch guilder to the euro. People in the city of Maastricht celebrated the changeover with fireworks.

Luxembourg, the Netherlands, Portugal, Spain, Sweden, and the United Kingdom. More are likely to join as the Union develops greater economic and political strength. Growth will create a more completely united Europe.

Headquartered in Brussels, Belgium, the EU has moved beyond trade agreements to promoting greater cooperation among its member nations in two additional areas: military and foreign policy, and law enforcement and immigration. Together with trade, these constitute the Union's three pillars of unity. To achieve its mission and to be responsive to changes in the world situation, the EU has created five governmental divisions to carry out its executive, legislative, and judicial functions. Each has a clearly defined responsibility, with the

15 member nations participating equally. This is how the framework is structured:

- The European Council is the key political body establishing the goals of the Union. It consists of the heads of state of the member nations with each one serving a six-month term as the president.

- The European Commission proposes policies and legislation to the European Council ensuring that the provisions of the many treaties defining the role of the EU are implemented.

- The Council of Ministers approves or rejects legislation from the European Commission and manages the Union's economic and trade policies. Its members are cabinet officers in their home countries.

- The European Parliament has 600 representatives, each elected for a 5-year term by the people of the EU's member nations. Their role is to debate proposals presented by the European Commission and to advise the Council of Ministers. The Parliament also approves the budget.

- The European Court of Justice is the equivalent of the Supreme Court in the United States. Its nine judges interpret EU law, and determine the legality of the decisions and actions of the other EU bodies. Its decisions are binding.

Since its inception at the end of the twentieth century, the European Union has become one of the world's largest trading partners, and is a leading force in the global economy. As a major player, the Netherlands can only continue to benefit from its participation as the Union expands and its sphere of influence widens.

The Dutch are proud of the products they create. These men pose with the huge wheels of cheese for which the town of Gouda is famous.

7

Living in the Netherlands

Over the centuries, the Dutch have developed an ordered and disciplined lifestyle reflective of a people who are industrious and practical. One commentator noted that the Netherlands is primarily an urban nation. However, one finds the same values and qualities in the countryside, only in a more tranquil setting. Throughout the Netherlands, the same traits prevail: an appreciation for comfortable and cozy homes, a pride in hard work, a commitment to family life, and a tolerance for divergent points of view. Some would also say that the Dutch have an obsession with the weather. Regardless of season, they talk about it constantly. Indeed, because of their precarious location and the country's history of flooding disasters, their concern is understandable. Life in such an unforgiving and unpredictable environment has given the Dutch a practical, no-nonsense outlook with an emphasis on facts and analysis instead of a reliance on subjective feelings.

A PILLARED SOCIETY

The Dutch enjoy a great sense of social equality. They value privacy and dislike flamboyance, displays of wealth, and personal extravagance. Such traits are offensive because they are viewed as being disruptive to the stability of society. This sense of egalitarianism (equality) has it roots on a long-cherished social tradition. The Dutch call it *verzuiling*, meaning "pillarization." Under this system, society is divided into pillars, or groups, each independent of the others. The pillars are Catholic, Protestant, socialist, and conservative. Traditionally, people have seen themselves belonging to one pillar or another. Each has had its own view of life promoted through its schools, clubs, labor unions, political parties, and universities. It was within each group that opinions developed so that collectively the pillars could support the larger Dutch society.

Over the years, the pillar concept has served as the foundation of Dutch life. It recognized that every person has a place, that all opinions should be heard, and that from the resulting ongoing dialogue, consensus can develop within a structure of harmony and order. The pillarization of society allowed people to be different yet equal. In recent years, however, verzuiling has changed as Dutch society has become more fluid and families more mobile. It still exists, but only in less obvious ways than in the past. The presence of increasing numbers of immigrants and a resistance on the part of younger people to the old social order are also responsible for its decline. Nonetheless, it has cast a long shadow. The power of its influence, even though diminished, continues to shape Dutch social values resulting in a remarkable level of tolerance for different lifestyles.

EDUCATION

The people of the Netherlands place a high priority on quality schooling. Their technological and service-oriented economy requires a well-educated population prepared to work either at home or in Dutch businesses abroad. At 99 percent, their literacy rate is among the highest in the world. All schools are publicly supported, even if they are religious institutions. The government's philosophy is that subsidies are directed at preparing young people for productive adult lives regardless of their religious affiliation. According to this viewpoint, public money directly aids the students, not the schools themselves.

School is compulsory for everyone between the ages of four and fifteen. Emphasis in the pre-school and early primary grades is on basic subjects, such as reading, writing, and mathematics. By grade four, the curriculum broadens to include the study of the Dutch language, science, geography, and history. Later, all students receive instruction in English, since the Dutch recognize that it has become the international language. An understanding of the English language enables those who work in the global economy to communicate easily.

When students enter high school, a national examination system helps identify how their schooling will continue. Some students go on to four-year programs in general or vocational education. Others are directed to the six-year pre-university program, a more competitive and specialized course of study preparing students for college admissions. High schools generally require foreign language training (especially English) and are roughly the equivalent to the first two years of an American college.

The Dutch university system is one of the oldest in the world, dating to the Middle Ages. It offers a variety of study opportunities in the humanities, physical and social sciences, technology and engineering, as well as medicine, law, and education. Students begin studies in their fields of specialization as freshmen. Course programs last from five to eight years. Of the country's 13 institutions of higher learning, only three are church-affiliated.

In recent decades, Dutch education has moved away from a fact-based experience where students memorize information in order to provide the correct answers on tests. Instead, it is preparing them to broaden their interests and helping students to become creative thinkers and effective problem solvers. Teachers encourage students to use a variety of resources, from print materials to the Internet, to formulate complex questions and develop innovative answers. Dutch teachers recognize that the world is growing more complex. Because it is impossible to know everything, the Dutch educational system is promoting alternative methods of teaching and learning. It is reaching beyond the traditional textbook and multiple-choice test to experiences and case studies based on real-life situations.

DEALING WITH CONTROVERSIAL ISSUES

As is true in all modern industrialized societies, there are a number of controversial topics that confront the people of the Netherlands. Dutch solutions to these problems sometimes elicit fierce international criticism because they appear to be out of step with the way other countries approach such issues. One example is the policy toward euthanasia, the medical practice of assisting the termination of a human life. The legislation regulating this practice is reflective of Dutch social values and results from the strong feelings of many citizens. They argue that when a person is terminally ill and in great pain, the patient should be the person to decide when to die.

Legislation permitting euthanasia was extensively debated with a rational examination of all the pros and cons in the media, the States-General, and public forums all over the country. The discussions were a search for a humane and acceptable solution of how to comfort people living out their final days in terrible pain. The outcome in the parliament did not make euthanasia legal in the Netherlands.

The Dutch can be extremely outspoken about political and social issues. These protesters carried on a demonstration outside the States-General while the politicians inside debated the legalization of euthanasia.

Instead, it established that those practicing euthanasia will not be prosecuted as long as they follow a set of strict conditions. The law stipulates that a terminally ill patient must assert that he or she wants to end life. Additionally, two physicians must independently agree. Finally, when a physician assists a patient in dying, it must be reported to the medical authorities for clinical judgment and registration, not legal prosecution.

The policy on euthanasia was implemented in 2000. Since then, the experience has been that most doctors urge their patients to continue to endure their suffering in a dignified manner with as much comfort as can be provided. If the patient insists that he or she wants to die, however, the doctor administers the life-ending drugs to bring about a painless death.

Dutch policy on drugs is another widely misunderstood issue. Contrary to reports, no drug is officially legal in the Netherlands. As with euthanasia, and perhaps deliberately so, the law pertaining to drugs is confusing and unclear. There is a legal prohibition against all drug use, but at the same time the law turns a blind eye to the use of some drugs, especially marijuana. There is no tolerance for use of so-called "hard-drugs," such as cocaine, crack, and heroin. Drug users are considered medical cases and not criminals. Drug addicts are helped through counseling and rehabilitation programs. Dealing in hard drugs is illegal and those caught are prosecuted. This is especially true in cases involving large-scale dealings in the international drug trade.

Tobacco use is another issue that the Dutch are trying to confront in a positive and tolerant manner. Smoking has been common in Dutch culture for hundreds of years. It is part of the colonial heritage; Dutch traders brought tobacco from Virginia plantations and the drying sheds of Caribbean islands. In recent years, however, there has been a dramatic decrease in tobacco use, largely as a result of government efforts to educate the population on the hazards of smoking. In the 1960s, about 90 percent of the male population smoked regularly. Now it is below 40 percent and continuing to decline. With women, however, the line has been flat at about 30 percent over the years. Many anti-tobacco groups blame the government for a half-hearted and inconsistent policy. As in other areas of society, though, the Dutch approach is a tolerant "live and let-live" attitude.

SCHOLARSHIP, INVESTIGATION, AND INVENTION: A RECORD OF ACHIEVEMENT

Few people in Europe have been more creative or visionary than the Dutch. The extent of their influence has been world-wide, touching the lives of millions of people. Their curiosity has led to extraordinary discoveries in all areas of human inquiry.

Among the most prominent and best known is Desiderius Erasmus (1466?–1536), a humanist whose research and writings made him one of the most respected people of his time. Although born in Rotterdam, he spent most of his life traveling and studying in other parts of Europe. He numbered kings, statesmen, poets, and popes within his circle of friends. One of the most notable of these friends was Henry VIII, the English monarch who separated his kingdom from the Catholic Church in Rome and named himself leader of the Church of England.

Erasmus, who studied at the University of Paris to become a priest, remained loyal to the Roman Catholic Church throughout his life. He worked earnestly to persuade such reformers as Martin Luther to change the Church from within and to avoid war and the cultural disruptions caused by the religious upheaval of the time. He failed to persuade them, however. The reformers argued that the Catholic Church had grown too corrupt to be saved. Erasmus wrote *In Praise of Folly* (1509), using his delicate writing style and sharp wit to try to persuade his critics to abandon their intolerance and work to restore order to Europe, which was being torn apart by religious warfare. His many contributions included translating the Bible into Latin from the original Greek and presenting updated editions of Greek and Latin classics. Despite the great esteem in which he was held for his lifetime of scholarly works, Erasmus is best remembered for his humanism and his efforts to heal the chasm between the Catholics and the Protestants. However, his humanist spirit, which urged conciliation and compromise between Catholics and Protestants, failed to stem the tide of the Reformation.

Hugo Grotius (1583–1645) was also a humanist in the tradition of Erasmus. A student at the University of Leiden, he became a lawyer when he was only 15 years old. Soon after, however, he was imprisoned for life because of a political wrangle. After a daring escape, he sought refuge in France, where he wrote the first comprehensive book on international law. The success of the book made him a renowned jurist. He based much of his book on the Bible and on the history of ancient Greece and Rome, arguing that common sense and natural law should guide the rules of conduct for nations as well as individuals. He also condemned war as a way to resolve disputes and urged it be used sparingly and only as a last resort. Later in his life, Grotius returned to Holland, but once again was forced to leave for political reasons. Today, he is remembered as the Father of International Law.

In the realms of science and mathematics, Christian Huygens (1629–1695) and Antony van Leeuwenhoek (1632–1723) made enduring contributions that not only broadened knowledge about life on Earth, but also provided startling glimpses of the universe. Huygens improved the telescope to such a degree that he discovered the rings of Saturn and one of its moons as well. This success led him to experiment with light waves and the refraction of light. His work laid the foundation for improved lenses that encouraged further astronomical investigations. Huygens was also the first to use a pendulum in a clock, making the calculation of time far more accurate than it had ever been.

Leeuwenhoek's work, on the other hand, focused on the mysterious domain of the human body. Because of his interest in microscopes, which he made increasingly more powerful, he discovered microorganisms that allowed him to be the first ever to provide complete descriptions of bacteria, protozoa, and spermatozoa. His ability to use his homemade microscopes to magnify things as much as 270 times their normal size allowed Leeuwenhoek to make detailed studies of red blood cells in his research on the circulatory system.

The lure of the unknown has attracted many Dutch over the centuries. Whether they sail to distant ports or study the far reaches of the universe, Dutch explorers have made great scientific discoveries. The achievements of the past challenge the present generation of the Netherlands to invent a promising future that will continue to be reflective of their rich history and solid values.

The Dutch face a promising but uncertain future. Finding a way to maintain their prosperity will be one of the primary challenges for the next generation.

8

The Netherlands Looks Ahead

A s the Netherlands moves into the twenty-first century, the
Dutch face many challenges and opportunities. For example,
they must find ways to continue their commercial success as
a leading economic power in the family of nations. Challenges also
exist that threaten Dutch identity and the stability that has characterized life in the Netherlands for centuries. Although it continues to
be a country of promise, there are signs of peril. Two difficult and
overarching questions face the Dutch. The first question focuses on
how the Dutch can build on the prosperity that has led them to the
pinnacle of business and trade. The second question concerns how
the Dutch can constructively address the social and environmental
problems they face that, if badly managed, will likely send the country
into a decline from which it is never likely to recover.

The ways the country chooses to approach these questions, and the issues surrounding them, will determine its future as a nation state. The years ahead are high-stakes times for the Dutch, as well as for their European neighbors who also face similar problems.

THE UNCERTAIN COSTS OF EUROPEAN UNITY

The Netherlands stands firmly committed to the mission of the European Union and supports the peacekeeping goals of the United Nations. In fact, it regularly contributes soldiers and money for peacekeeping in faraway countries. In addition, the Netherlands has been one of the most generous contributors of money to relief efforts, human rights initiatives, and ecological projects worldwide. The Dutch see this as one of the country's responsibilities as a world citizen. Active involvement in the European Union and the United Nations is an important part of the country's foreign policy and is viewed as essential for their survival.

The Netherlands has promoted European cooperation since 1945. Still, doubts sometime surface as a unified Europe becomes more of a reality. Some people express concerns about the euro replacing the guilder, open national boundaries allowing people to freely cross from one country to another, and the absence of tariffs that once protected Dutch business from foreign competition. The leaders of the European Union are beginning to play as important a role in Dutch policy-making as are the leaders of the Netherlands in The Hague. There are other doubts as well. What results is a nagging awareness that being "European" seems to be replacing the importance of being "Dutch."

Many of the changes brought about by European unity have benefited the economy of the Netherlands. Other changes, however, have proved troublesome because of their social implications. Where will they lead? Can Dutch culture—their way of life—be safeguarded? Can the Dutch language and Dutch institutions survive in the long run? What about the Dutch flag, the monarchy, the national anthem, and all else that is special to the people of the Netherlands? The ultimate question, then, becomes whether European unity is worth the risk of losing institutions that define Dutch nationality and identity.

There are no immediate answers. Dutch society is changing rapidly. So is its worldview. As always, however, the determination of the Dutch will help them forge a bright future in Europe and beyond.

ENVIRONMENTAL ISSUES

Of all the European countries, the Netherlands is the most environmentally proactive. It was the first to frame a national policy on sustainable development to assure that city and suburban expansion would meet high standards and maintain as much of the beauty of the landscape as possible. The Netherlands also implemented plans to protect precious farmland from the ravages of unchecked growth. The policy's larger purpose has been to organize planning strategies using advanced technologies. For example, Geographic Information Systems (GIS) and remote sensing are being used to determine the most efficient means of using space for homes and parks, as well as roads, railroad networks, and improved port and harbor facilities.

Pollution has long been a Dutch concern, with aggressive efforts now in place to curb its impact on the water supply and air quality. Acid rain has been particularly troublesome, affecting a significantly high percentage of the country's trees. Much of this pollution originates elsewhere, especially in the industrial regions of Germany and the United Kingdom. The situation is improving, however, due to directives from the European Union and the UN Economic Commission for Europe (ECE). Both have been effective regulating the use of the environment.

The fragile North Sea coast poses a constant concern for the Dutch. With major petroleum finds off the coast of Norway, and growing numbers of sea-based drilling rigs

Pollution is one of the most pressing issues facing the Netherlands and there are strong efforts in place to curb its impact on air and water.

between Norway and the Scottish coast, oil spills are always a threat. Tanker traffic to and from Rotterdam's refineries also increases the risk. In the ugly world of oil spills, high-tech ships designed to suck up hundreds of tons of petroleum a day are the first line of defense. They provide the key to keeping the muck at bay when disaster strikes. Their cabins glow with computer screens, radar, and satellite positioning gear as they track the black goo and keep their suction pumps whining like buzz saws, night and day.

With almost 60 percent of the population living below sea level, the Netherlands is particularly vulnerable to the impact of global warming. If the world's average temperature continues to increase, as many scientists suggest it will, polar ice caps and mountain glaciers will continue to melt. This melting water will, in turn, cause the levels of the oceans to rise. A rising sea level would have disastrous consequences for the Dutch, regardless of the height and strength of their dams and dikes. Because of this environmental threat, the Dutch have led the campaign to reduce fossil-fuel use and end deforestation in the tropical rain forests. Holland itself contributes less than 1 percent of global greenhouse emissions, making it one of the few nonpolluters among the world's nations.

POPULATION PRESSURES

With over 16 million people, the Netherlands is one of the most densely populated nations in the world. Actual crowding is even greater, because more than half the people live on only 15 percent of the land. Density, however, does not necessarily mean overpopulation. The constructive use of space determines the quality of life in a country. Taiwan and Hong Kong also have dense populations. Like the Netherlands, however, careful planning has saved them from the negative impact of too many people occupying too little space. In Holland, concentrations are in the urban neighborhoods of the Randstad, where densities soar well beyond 1,000 inhabitants per square mile. Polders have been created to ease crowding, but land continues to be scarce as the demand constantly increases.

Urban planners in the Netherlands are experimenting with innovative techniques to respond to the growing space needs of the population. One is a recent invention called "The City of the Future." Known as *Nieuwland*, it is a neighborhood subdivision of 600 homes and businesses within the city of Amersfoort, an industrial and food processing center about one hour's drive from Amsterdam. Designed as a model utilizing solar energy, new construction materials, innovative building methods, and striking planning for public places such as schools, parks, and squares, it is a window on tomorrow. Jointly funded by the Dutch government and the European Union, Nieuwland's designers aim to provide an urban habitat that captures the subtle balance between modernity and the living style common to the Dutch.

Population growth has fallen sharply since World War II, with recent increases averaging only about 1 percent annually. This may seem low, but a number of European countries have achieved a rate of zero population growth (ZPG). The population of some countries, such as Germany and Italy, are actually decreasing! With fewer children being born in Holland, the population has grown older. Presently, only one in four people is under 15 years old. In the mid-1950s, about half the people of the Netherlands were under 15 years old. On the other hand, the percentage of those 65 or older is on the increase, with costs for pensions, health care, and senior housing rising as well.

Movement in and out of the country has been a significant factor in Dutch population trends in recent decades. After World War II, many Dutch citizens left permanently for Canada, the United States, or Australia because these countries were less impacted by the devastation of the war. In the last half of the twentieth century, emigration and immigration in the Netherlands fluctuated depending upon economic conditions and job availability.

After Indonesian independence in 1949, more than 200,000 Dutch nationals returned to the Netherlands to take up permanent residence. By the 1960s, job opportunities were expanding so rapidly that the country suffered a labor shortage and invited Italians, Spaniards, Turks, and people from the Caribbean and North Africa to come as "guest workers." Although these were meant to be temporary job placements, many workers decided to stay and sought permanent residence along with their families. By 1980, there were 400,000 foreigners living in the Netherlands.

THE CHALLENGES OF IMMIGRATION

In recent years, the Dutch have begun to rethink their immigration policy. Growing unemployment in lower paying jobs, plus a reduction in the expectations for economic growth, have caused some Dutch politicians to proclaim that "the ship

The Netherlands is a leader in international aid. These workers are loading a Dutch airplane with relief goods destined for a refugee camp in Pakistan.

is full." Estimates are that up to 15 percent of the population is not native born. About half are people from former colonies who already have Dutch citizenship. The exact number is not known because of legal restrictions on registering race or ethnicity. The remaining are an estimated 300,000 residents of Turkish origin and 250,000 Moroccans living in the Netherlands. Asylum seekers have come from Afghanistan, Iraq, Sudan, Somalia, the former Yugoslavia, Angola, Iran, and Sierra Leone. The government's challenge is to check on the validity of their claims to determine who should be admitted into the country.

As an indication of the growing concern over the presence of a foreign population in the country, the Dutch government has created a new agency known as the Ministry of Large

Cities Policy and Integration. This agency assists non-Dutch residents with their everyday problems. At the same time, the government has announced border patrols to track down and deport undocumented asylum seekers and illegal immigrants. Recent estimates suggest that as many as 100,000 people enter the Netherlands unofficially each year. Many of these people are fleeing poverty, war, and social disorder in their home countries.

With serious tensions developing, especially in the crowded cities where there are numerous immigrant enclaves, arguments for restrictive immigration policies are an increasingly common topic on the political agenda. Historically, there has been little discussion concerning immigrant communities. In fact until recently, it was never even identified as a problem, but that is changing. Anti-immigrant rhetoric is becoming more common.

WHAT NEXT?

Dutch society has become much more complex in recent years, as ethnic minorities appear in increasingly greater numbers. According to estimates, they constitute about 5 percent of the population. Even in such a traditionally open society, respect for diversity can become strained. Pluralism once treasured, can turn tolerance to indifference and even intolerance. Today, Dutch and non-Dutch alike must learn to deal with the frustrations of unemployment, which sometimes results in vandalism, drug dealing, theft, and other crime.

If the openness and cultural acceptance that has so long characterized Dutch society holds, the final outcome of its growing multiculturalism is more likely to be integration rather than disintegration. It is almost certain that the great majority of second and third generation immigrants and asylum seekers will learn the Dutch language, reach higher levels of education, intermarry, and qualify for better jobs. If the global economy continues to grow and the Dutch prosper, it is likely that over the next decades the family names of Turks,

Iranians, Moroccans, and the other ethnic groups will be just as accepted as French and German names are now. It is also likely that the features of Africans, Asians, and South Americans will become as commonplace as being "just plain Dutch." Among the multiple strengths of the Dutch have been their adaptability and their resilience in the face of change.

Facts at a Glance

Land and People

Official Name of Country	Kingdom of the Netherlands
Popular Name of Country	Holland
Location	Northwestern Europe along the coast of the North Sea between Belgium and Germany
Area	15,768 square miles (40,839 square kilometers), slightly larger than Maryland
Percent Urban	89% (United States: 76%)
Capitals	Amsterdam (administrative center) The Hague (seat of government)
Other Major Cities	Rotterdam, Tilburg, Eindhoven, Utrecht, Groningen
Major Rivers	Rhine, Maas, Scheldt
Climate	Temperate
Population	16,067,754 (July 2002 est.)
Population Density	1,018 per square mile (2,637 per square kilometer) (United States: 79 per square mile)
Official Languages	Dutch and Frisian
Literacy Rate	99%
Religions	Roman Catholic 31%, Protestant 21%, Muslim 4%, other 4%, unspecified 40%
Average Life Expectancy	78.5 years
Overseas Dependencies	Aruba and the Netherlands Antilles
National Flag	Red, white, and blue horizontal stripes

Economy

Natural Resources	Natural gas, oil, arable land, waterpower
Agricultural Products	Sheep, cattle, pigs, goats, poultry, fish, grains, potatoes, sugar beets, vegetables, flowers, flower bulbs
Industries	Machinery, chemicals, oil refining, microelectronics, tourism
Major Imports	Consumer goods, processed foods, transportation equipment, petroleum
Major Exports	Agricultural products, processed foods, flowers, flower bulbs, natural gas, chemicals
Major Trading Partners	European Union
Currency	Euro (formerly the guilder)
Per Capita Gross Domestic Product (GDP)	$23,100 (2002)

Government

Form of Government	Parliamentary democracy under a constitutional monarchy
Government Bodies	States General
Formal Head of State	Queen or King
Head of Government	Prime Minister
Voting Rights	Universal suffrage at age 18 years
Date of Independence	September 18, 1830 (after the Brussels Revolution)

History at a Glance

300 B.C.	Germanic and Celtic tribes move into the area south of the Rhine River
1st century B.C.	Romans conquer tribes in northwestern Europe
A.D. 400s	German tribes invade from the east with Franks dominating; conversion to Christianity begins
800	Charlemagne crowned, establishes Holy Roman Empire, and controls Low Countries (including the Netherlands)
1400s	Renaissance and Humanism take root in the prosperous cities of the Netherlands
1555–79	Spanish troops occupy the Netherlands after many Dutch convert to Protestantism
1581	United Provinces declared, making the Netherlands an independent country
1602	Dutch East India Company founded
1609	Independence of Holland from Spain resulting in the formation of the United Provinces
1652	Dutch maritime wars with England begin
1668	Dutch ally with Britain and Sweden against France to consolidate power
1795	Napoleon takes over Belgium and the Netherlands
1813	French withdraw from the Netherlands
1814	William I of the House of Orange becomes first monarch of the United Kingdom of the Netherlands; constitution written establishing a constitutional monarchy
1830	Belgium gains independence from the Netherlands
1914–1918	The Netherlands remains neutral during World War I
1940	Germany invades the Netherlands during World War II
1957–86	Delta Plan developed curbing the power of the Rhine delta and the North Sea due to disastrous floods in 1953

1999 Treaty of Maastricht negotiated as a key step toward the establishment of the European Union (EU)

2002 The Netherlands converts currency to the euro replacing the guilder as the medium of exchange

Further Reading

Bailey, Donna. *Netherlands* (Where We Live Series). Steck-Vaughn Library, 1992.

Bennett, Linda A., ed. *Encyclopedia of World Cultures*. G. K. Hall, 1992.

Catling, Christopher. *Amsterdam* (Insight Guides). APA Press, 1991.

Cummings, David. *The Netherlands* (Our Country Series). The Bookwright Group Press, 1992.

Fraden, Dennis B. *The Netherlands* (Enchantment of the World Series). Children's Press, 1983.

Hintz, Marin. *The Netherlands* (Enchantment of the World Series). Children's Press, 1999.

Netherlands in Pictures (Visual Geography Series). Lerner Publications, 1991.

Ozer, Steve. *The Netherlands* (Places and People of the World Series). Chelsea House Publishers, 1990.

Seward, Pat. *Netherlands*. Marshall, 1995.

CIA World Fact Book 2000
http://www.cia.doe.gov/emeu/publications/factbook/index.html

European Union
http://www.eurunion.org/profile/brief.htm

Goode's World Atlas, 20th ed. Rand McNally, 2000.

The Kingdom of the Netherlands
http://www.nisnews.nl/neth/htm

Merriam Webster Geographical Dictionary, 3rd ed. Springfield: Merriam-Webster Incorporated, 1998.

Vossistein, Jacob. *Dealing with the Dutch*. KIT Publishers, 2001.

White, Colin and Laurie Boucke. *The Undutchables, An Observation of The Netherlands: Its Culture and Its Inhabitants.* Lafayette, CO: White Boucke Publications, 1993.

Index

Index

Index

page:

8: New Millennium Images
14: © 2003 Maps.com
16: New Millennium Images
20: © 2003 Maps.com
23: New Millennium Images
25: © Paul Almasy/Corbis
28: New Millennium Images
35: New Millennium Images
38: AP/Wide World Photos
40: New Millennium Images
45: New Millennium Images
50: New Millennium Images

52: © Bettmann/Corbis
57: Reuters/NMI
59: New Millennium Images
62: New Millennium Images
67: AFP/NMI
70: Frits Widdershoven/AP
72: New Millennium Images
77: Serge Ligtenberg/AP
82: New Millennium Images
86: © Syril Granet/Corbis Sygma
89: AFP/NMI

Cover: © Larry Lee Photography/Corbis

About the Author

JAMES F. MARRAN is Social Studies Chair Emeritus at New Trier Township High School, Winnetka, Illinois. Presently he is a curriculum consultant in social studies with a primary interest on issues in geographic education. Mr. Marran and his wife Barbara live in metro-Chicago.

CHARLES F. ("FRITZ") GRITZNER is Distinguished Professor of Geography at South Dakota University in Brookings. He is now in his fifth decade of college teaching and research. During his career, he has taught more than 60 different courses, spanning the fields of physical, cultural, and regional geography. In addition to his teaching, he enjoys writing, working with teachers, and sharing his love for geography with students. As consulting editor for the MODERN WORLD NATIONS series, he has a wonderful opportunity to combine each of these "hobbies." Fritz has served as both president and executive director of the National Council for Geographic Education and has received the Council's highest honor, the George J. Miller Award for Distinguished Service.